Your **BRILLIANT** CV

Full of great advice, guidance and examples to help you write brilliant CVs that will get you noticed and win you interviews.

This book is aimed at anyone wanting to write CVs, from Chief Executives through to someone applying for their first job.

By

Anna Sheather

Published by Élan Coaching Ltd

www.elancoaching.co.uk

Book cover design by Spiffing Covers Ltd

First published 2014

ISBN: 978-1-909425-75-0

ISBN: 978-1-909425-76-7 (.mobi)

ISBN: 978-1-909425-77-4 (.epub)

Coming Soon

Your ***Brilliant*** Interview

Your ***Brilliant*** Covering Letters & Emails

Your ***Brilliant*** Transferable Skills

Your ***Brilliant*** Career Goals

Your ***Brilliant*** Job Search

Your ***Brilliant*** Application Form

Your ***Brilliant*** Confidence

Contents

INTRODUCTION

Having coached a wide variety of people at all stages in their careers, I have now put my fingers to the keyboard to share my experiences with you. My clients have come from all walks of life, different industry sectors and different stages in their careers, from first jobs through to Chief Executives of multimillion-pound organisations. Many have suggested that I write books and so I have finally given in and done just that! I hope you find this booklet helpful and any others in the series that you use.

This booklet is part of the 'Your *Brilliant...*' series. I have written this series for anyone who is looking for advice and guidance on getting and securing their next role, whether it is their first role, a complete change of career direction or the next step on their career path. Each booklet covers a specific career-coaching topic and I have written them in this way so that you can pick and choose the support you need for your own career-coaching needs. Each booklet is designed for you to work through and coach yourself to career success!

Introduction to *Your Brilliant CV*

Advice and guidance on CVs can be found everywhere. You only have to type 'CV' into any internet search engine and you will come up with many thousands of sites all offering their take on what you should and shouldn't do to write a CV.

Why **brilliant**? Because with the help of this booklet your CV will:

1. highlight all your skills, knowledge, experience and capabilities that show you to be a **brilliant** candidate for that job
2. stand out **brilliantly** from the crowd, and
3. be **brilliantly** written.

It is CV overload! To help you cut through all of this, I have, in this booklet, brought together my years of experience in helping people at all levels to write professional, successful CVs. This booklet concentrates on the facts, providing you with lots of practical advice and guidance that has been tried and tested by my clients, thereby helping them to write brilliant CVs that get them interviews.

This booklet is relevant for anyone who wants to write and/or update their CV, whether you are a CEO of a multinational organisation or you are writing your very first CV. The principles of successful CV writing are the same.

In this booklet you will find:

- information on the different types of CV and their uses, including e-CVs
- advice and guidance on writing a *Brilliant* CV
- help with writing a style of *Brilliant* CV that works for many of my clients
- a CV checklist to help you write your own *Brilliant* CV
- some examples of real CVs
- tips on writing *Brilliant* covering letters.

To help you further with your CV, I have also put examples of each type of CV in Annex C of this booklet.

Good luck.

Anna

CHAPTER 1
THE PURPOSE OF YOUR BRILLIANT CV

Your CV has one purpose:

To get you an interview

To achieve this, your CV must be written with the reader in mind. This is because your CV and your covering letter are all the reader has to go on when making a decision about whether to invite you to an interview or not.

This is the same whether you are writing a CV for a specific job application or creating an on-line CV on a job-search site or with an employment agency.

The role of your CV is not only to convey how you meet the requirements of the job, but also to tell the reader something about you as a person. It is, therefore, important that your CV presents you in the best possible way, maximising your chances of getting through to the next stage of the selection process.

The person who is reviewing your CV will have many to look through, so yours must stand out from the crowd. It is important that your CV:

- ensures the reader can quickly and clearly see what they are looking for, and
- gives a good and lasting impression of you.

Stand out from the crowd

CVs are always required when applying for Private Sector jobs and are used more than application forms. For the Public Sector, application forms are often used more than CVs and if CVs are requested they can be shortened versions, as the application forms and additional information statements cover everything.

When a CV is required, it is important that the CV is written in a way that helps to sell you into the role. What style you use is up to you. However, how it is written and formatted is crucial if you are to grab the attention of the reader quickly, stand out from the crowd and get that interview.

CHAPTER 2
DIFFERENT TYPES OF CV AND WHEN TO USE THEM

This section provides an overview of the 4 well-known types of CV and their different purposes. These are the:

1. skills-based CV

2. chronological CV

3. hybrid CV

4. e-CV

1. The skills-based CV

The skills-based CV is exactly that; it is a CV written with the focus on your skills and experience rather than on your career history.

This style of CV focuses the reader's attention on the skills and experiences that you are bringing to the role, and allows them to make a judgement on your suitability as a candidate without being distracted by job-role titles and different industry or sector experiences, which may not be relevant to the role.

This form of CV is very useful if you are:

• looking to change direction in your career and want to take the attention off previous roles and focus prospective employers' attention on relevant transferable skills and experience

• wanting to change industry or sector and want to remove any prejudices and perceptions that may exist. For example, moving between the Private and Public Sectors

• wanting to downsize your career and don't want to draw attention to previous roles that may be perceived as too senior or too responsible for the role you are applying for

- applying for your first role and don't have a career history

- coming back into the job market after an absence

The first page of a skills-based CV provides a succinct profile of who you are as a professional person. This is then followed by a list of your relevant skills, tailored to the job you are applying for. These will be your transferable skills as well as your skills that are directly applicable to the role. Your skills also include your knowledge, experience and capabilities.

Each of your skills should be written in a credible way so that the reader feels confident that you **do** have those skills. Credibility is important as we can all list skills, but how will the reader know that what you say is backed up by real experience? Your potential employer is unlikely to invite you for interview unless you can prove your ability.

The best way to prove your ability is to provide an example of how you have used those skills to achieve something. One example per skill is all that would be required and your example should be something, if at all possible, that is relevant to the role and/or organisation. The example should show you in your best light – highlighting something that you are proud of, such as a key achievement.

The second page of a *skills-based CV* is where you would summarise your career/job history, education and professional training.

Chapter 3: Writing your Brilliant CV gives you lots of hints, tips and guidance on how to write your CV and an example of a skills-based CV can be found in Annex C of this booklet.

More information about transferable skills and changing career direction can be found in my booklet *Your Brilliant Transferable Skills*.

2. The chronological CV

The chronological CV is the opposite of the skills-based CV.

This CV focuses attention on your career and is best used when applying for a role that is either similar to, or a natural progression from, your current role. Using this CV focuses the reader's attention on your career and, in particular, your very relevant recent roles and your current role. This helps the reader to identify quickly and clearly your career history – your progression, the development of your experience and the responsibilities you have held.

This type of CV is ideal if you are:

• following a particular career path

• needing to demonstrate sound experience in a particular sector or industry.

As with the skills-based CV, this CV should start with a succinct profile of you as a professional person. This is then followed by your career history in chronological order, starting on page one with your latest position and then working backwards. For each of your roles, you should outline your key responsibilities in a succinct paragraph and follow it with between 3 and 5 bullet points of key achievements that you have accomplished in that role. This provides depth and credibility to your experience and enables the reader to evaluate your skills, knowledge and experience.

Chapter 3: Writing your Brilliant CV gives you lots of hints, tips and guidance on how to write your CV and an example of a chronological CV can be found in Annex C of this booklet.

3. The hybrid CV

This CV format has proved very successful for the people I coach and many employers like this style of CV. This is because it brings together the skills-based CV and the chronological CV, allowing a prospective employer to quickly identify if an applicant is a good candidate for the role.

I tend to use the *hybrid CV* for my clients rather than the *chronological CV.*

The hybrid CV is particularly beneficial when applying for a job where:

• it is **similar** to your current role

- you are **seeking promotion** in the same field as your current role

- you are applying for roles in the **same sector.**

As this is the most popular format of CV, you can find a detailed breakdown of how to write each part of this CV in *Chapter 5: A Brilliant CV style that works: the hybrid CV in more detail.*

Chapter 3: Writing your Brilliant CV also gives you lots of hints, tips and guidance on writing your CV.

An example of a hybrid CV can also be found in Annex C of this booklet.

The hybrid CV does not, however, replace the skills-based CV and I would still recommend the skills-based CV if you are looking to change careers or sectors, or if you are just starting out on your career.

4. The e-CV

The e-CV or electronic CV refers to a number of different types of CV. They are:

- CVs you submit electronically, attached to an email, and take the form of Word, pdf, MAC equivalent or other file format documents, the most common being Word and pdf documents. This will be your 2-page skills-based, chronological or hybrid CV

- CVs you upload into an employer's database or an employment agency's database via a webpage. Again this would be your skills-based, chronological or hybrid CV

- CV forms that you complete on a job website that make your CV information available for on-line searches and matches. Here you have to use the template provided and your information has to be fitted into the on-line database's requirements. Employment agencies can also have their own on-line forms.

In this on-line job-market world, you should at least have your CV in an electronic file format, such as a Word document or pdf document, and be able to attach it to emails, upload it to websites and know how to use on-line job sites. It is becoming less common for people to ask you to send in hard copy CVs.

Submitting electronic CV documents

Where you have written and created your CV in an electronic file for submission, you are in complete control of the content and the presentation of yourself through your CV. In these circumstances, it is important that your document arrives looking the same as when it left you. To ensure this happens, you should give yourself time to check and consider the following:

- Does the formatting of your CV stay the same when sending via email or uploading into an on-line database? Consider using a pdf version that protects the content and style of your CV.

- If you have used MAC software to create your CV and the organisation you are sending it to uses Windows, check your CV document will open okay in Windows before submitting it.

- Print out your CV on someone else's printer to make sure your version of the document prints out okay on other printers. For example, if you have written your CV on an earlier version of Windows, the formatting of your CV may change when printing from newer versions.

- Has the organisation asked you to attach your own document or has it asked for it in a different format? If an organisation is concerned about viruses infecting their system through external file attachments, it could ask you to send it in using a different format. For example, they may ask you to copy your CV into the actual email, using plain text. This will remove all formatting and you should review how it looks before sending it in, making sure it is as easy to read as possible. This can be very disappointing and frustrating when you have put all that effort into making your CV look great. However, everyone applying will have been asked to do the same, so you will not be at a disadvantage in terms of the presentation and style of your CV.

On-line job site and employment agency forms

Many people upload their CV details onto on-line job sites to receive notifications of job vacancies or to allow prospective employers to match their job vacancy details to your credentials.

When you do this, you are adding your details to a large database that enables searches to be done based on keywords and phrases. As matching between job seekers and recruiters is based on these very impersonal searches, it is important that you consider the following:

- **Be clear about what job you are looking for** – The more focused your CV details are on a particular kind of role, the more likely you are to be matched to roles you are interested in and receive notification of vacancies. This is because your CV will contain many words and phrases that allow a database to clearly match your information to specific roles. The more generic your CV, the less matches you are likely to receive as you will have diluted the words and phrases that databases rely on.

- **Multiple CVs** – If you are looking for a number of different opportunities to maximise your chances of securing a role, you should upload a CV for each type of role you are considering, tailoring each one to the role you are looking for.

- **Keywords** – When you are applying on-line for a specific job, it is important that you include all the keywords in the job description and/ or person specification. This ensures the database matches your e-CV and application to the role and you can be considered for interview. Using the keywords also enables you to demonstrate to the reader that you understand what is required of the job and you can demonstrate how your relevant skills and experience match their needs. This significantly increases your chances of being considered. For more information on how to write your CV in this way, read *Chapter 3: Writing Your Brilliant CV.*

- **Include examples of your relevant experience and skills** – This is vital if you are to show the prospective employer that you are a credible applicant. Your examples should include the keywords above

16

so that when the search engine finds the keywords, the reader will automatically read your examples. For more information on how to write your examples in a credible way, read *Chapter 3: Writing your Brilliant CV.*

Some words of caution with e-CVs

There are a couple of areas that you need to think about regarding e-CVs:

- **Multiple entries** – The quality of your on-line entries matters. Above, I mentioned that if you are looking for a variety of options then you should upload tailored CVs for each type of role you are looking for. However, where this may backfire is where you upload the same CV to multiple job sites and/or employment agency sites. This is because a potential employer may use more than one site and your name may keep cropping up, giving an impression of desperation. If your CV is very good and matches well, then this is okay as the employer will have a positive view of your credibility and ability to do the role. However, if your CV is not great and it keeps popping up, it will just further underline the employer's more negative impression of you. Even if you upload a really good one later, as soon as they see your name they will almost certainly not look at it, believing it to be the previous CV. So it is really important that the quality of CV you put out there is very high.

- **Printed CVs from e-CV sites** – Sometimes people may want to print off your application/e-CV so that they can read it off-line and compare it to others they may have received. As the process of writing an e-CV doesn't always provide you with an opportunity to format it in a reader-friendly way, it is important that you take advantage of any formatting flexibility that the on-line database you are using allows, for example, creating space between paragraphs, the use of bullets to break up large areas of text, using bold or underlining headings and so forth. More hints and tips on how to write your skills and experience in a reader-friendly way are in the next chapter.

CHAPTER 3
WRITING YOUR BRILLIANT CV

In this chapter you will find lots of advice, guidance, hints and tips on how to approach writing your *Brilliant CV.* This is based on all the information that my clients have found very helpful and useful for writing their own CVs.

This chapter focuses on writing the standard 2-page CV, whether *skills-based, chronological* or *hybrid*. Many of the points are also relevant to completing an on-line e-CV or e-CV form.

You will also find additional hints and tips in Chapter 5 where I go through writing the hybrid CV in more detail.

As we have already stated, the purpose of the CV is to get you an interview. You only need to provide enough information to grab the attention of the reader so they want to find out more about you and your suitability for the role. The reader wants to be able to match their requirements to your CV quickly and easily, enabling them to make a decision to interview you.

Always write your CV with the reader in mind

So how do you write a CV that grabs the reader's attention? What will they be looking for?

Put yourself in their shoes…

The applications are coming in (email, on-line or even the post bag) and you have a pile of CVs to read. If the vacancy is popular this could be in the hundreds. How are you going to get through them all? How are you going to be feeling after reading just the first 20? What selection and filtering criteria are you putting in place to help you get through them all quickly?

It makes you think, doesn't it?

How can we help the reader and make sure we maximise our chances of being put in the interview pile?

By following the advice and guidance below, you can write a professional, *Brilliant CV* that maximises your chances of getting an interview.

Writing your *Brilliant* CV

In this section, I will cover how to approach your CV and write it professionally. It includes:

1. The structure and format of your *Brilliant* CV

2. Tailoring your CV to the job

3. Being *Brilliant* and standing out from the crowd

4. Covering gaps in knowledge, skills and experience

5. Before you send your *Brilliant* CV in...

1. The structure and format of your *Brilliant* CV

How you lay out your CV will be crucial to helping the reader see what they are looking for quickly and easily. For examples of structures, see the CV examples in Annex C of this booklet.

When somebody reads a CV, they will first be drawn to the top third of your first page. If they read something of interest here they will then scan and maybe read the rest of your first page. They may then look at and scan your second page. Few people read the second page in detail when doing an initial sorting of CVs. This may seem unfair but it is human nature and everyone gets treated the same.

Understanding how someone reads a document helps you to lay out your CV for maximum impact. It is why – for the skills-based, chronological and hybrid CVs – we recommend opening up with a profile. Well-written, your profile grabs the reader's attention and encourages them to continue reading. It is also why the hybrid CV works well, as your profile is followed by a summary of your key skills, which shows the reader how you match the job requirements.

Key points:

- Your CV should be no longer than 2 pages of A4 unless the job application requirement states something different. Make the most of your 2 pages. Be succinct and to the point. Every word should convey something about you and your experience.

- Put your name in the header of your document so it automatically appears on both pages. This ensures that, if your CV is printed out, your CV pages won't get separated.

- Put your contact details at the top of page 1 so they can easily be found. It doesn't need to go in the header. Your contact details should include your address, telephone number (home, work, mobile – depending on which ones you would like them to contact you on) and an appropriate email address.

- The **style and size of font** you use should be easy to read. Avoid using too many different styles and sizes of font as your CV may end up looking messy and make it harder for people to read. It may also give a negative impression of you.

- The **use of colour** should also be used with care. This may be different if you are writing a CV for a more creative role where colour may convey a more creative person. The norm would be to use black fonts or dark greys, which may be varied with blue or shades of grey. If you are using colours or greys, make sure it prints clearly and doesn't appear too pale.

- Break up **blocks of text** by using space between paragraphs and the different sections of your CV, as well as using bullet points. This will make your CV much easier on the eye and easier to read.

- Use **bold text** for headings and to highlight the occasional keyword. This helps the reader navigate their way around your CV, finding what they want quickly and, as importantly, what you want them to read! However, too much bold becomes messy and confusing, so use it sparingly.

- You should show the **dates of your employment** for each role, the dates when you qualified for your profession and the dates when you were in education. These dates only need to be the years. For example, if you were in Human Resources you may have been an HR Administrator between November 2008 and March 2010. You would show your dates as 2008 to 2010.

- Prospective employers review dates for continuity and gaps. To help the reader do this quickly, I recommend that dates are put down the right-hand side of the CV (see examples in Annex C). If you prefer, they can be put down the left-hand side but, whichever you choose, make sure you are consistent. If you have gaps in your dates of employment, *Chapter 4: Brilliant tips to deal with common issues with CVs* has ideas on how to address them.

Contact Information Tips:

Email: Check your email address. If you are using a family address, just make sure it is something sensible. For example, yummymummy4@ themadhouse.net may not be giving the impression you want to give to a prospective employer! If this sounds familiar, think about opening a Hotmail or Google or other generic email account.

Voicemail: If you are giving personal phone numbers as contact details, it may be worth checking your home and mobile phone voicemail messages that callers hear!

Facebook: Could a prospective employer get access to you or your family's Facebook page? If they could, what would it say about you? Employers are increasingly looking here for information on applicants.

Twitter: If you have a Twitter account, what would it tell a prospective employer about you if they signed up to follow you?

Have a look at the examples in Annex C for more ideas on the structure of a CV.

- **a photo** of yourself unless it is a specific requirement of the application

- your **date of birth, age, sex** and **marital status.**

2. Tailoring your CV to the job

Tailoring your CV to the job may seem like common sense but I am always amazed at how many people send the same CV in, no matter what the role or organisation. If you do this:

- the reader will find it difficult to match their requirements to your CV

- you will come across as disinterested in the job and the organisation as you have given the impression that you haven't time to read the job requirements and check you are a good candidate for the role

- you will not have built up any rapport between you and the reader

- you may even come across as arrogant

- you are unlikely to get an interview.

1. Read the role requirements fully.
2. Identify the key requirements.
3. If you don't understand something, ask!
4. Match your skills, experience and knowledge to the key requirements.

It is absolutely vital that you tailor your CV each time you apply for a job. This may be a small adjustment for some applications and a bigger change for others. It all depends on the role and what the organisation is looking for. We all have a variety of skills and experience that can be presented in many different ways. To maximise your chances of getting an interview, it is important that you present yourself in a way that best matches what the prospective employer is looking for. To do this:

i. Read the role requirements fully

These requirements will be found in the job advertisement and job description. In addition, there may be a person specification, additional papers and on-line links for more information on the organisation and/or the department the job is in. For senior roles you may also have organisational strategies, business plans and accounting information.

It is important that you do as much research around the job as possible as this will tell you what skills, experience, capabilities and personal attributes they are looking for in a candidate.

ii. Identify the key requirement

Having done your research, it is now time to identify the key requirements of the role. Here you are looking for the keywords and phrases that identify the main experiences, skills and capabilities required from a candidate. Sometimes the job advertisement outlines what you need to address in your application. For example, they may ask you to send in a CV and covering letter, showing how you meet the requirements set out in the person specification or job description.

iii. If you don't understand something, ask!

I have lost count of the times I have been working with someone on their CV only to discover they have written it without actually understanding some of the requirements.

If you find yourself saying, 'I think it means...', 'I am sure it is...', 'I believe it is...', 'I presume that...' or 'I assume that...', STOP! You are about to apply for a job based on assumptions. Your assumptions may be right, but what if they are wrong?

If there are things you don't understand or are not sure of, ask! Most job advertisements have a contact number or email you can use to ask clarification questions.

If the prospect of ringing up beforehand fills you with dread, or you are concerned the organisation may think badly of you for not understanding something, think again. Firstly, ringing up and asking a few well-thought-out clarification questions shows you are proactive and confident. Secondly, would you rather miss an opportunity by making assumptions, or increase your chances of an interview by ensuring your application really does meet their requirements?

The key is for your questions to be well thought out so you ring up once, or twice at the very most, and ensure you come across clearly and get the answers you need. If the contact person can't help you, ask who can. If they say they are not able to give you the contact details, you will have to find another way to answer your questions. Does the website give any clues? Do you know anyone in the organisation or someone who used to work there who could help? Think creatively!

iv. Match your skills, experience and knowledge to the key requirements

The next stage is to match your skills, experience, knowledge and personal attributes to the key requirements. It isn't good enough to say that you match them; you must demonstrate this through examples of your work.

If you already have a CV, it may just be a case of changing the emphasis of what is already there, re-ordering skills and key achievements and changing certain words and phrases so they match the requirements.

What you write must be in your own language, so don't just paraphrase what is in the job description and/or person specification, make it your own.

How you write this part of your CV will help you stand out from the crowd. See *Section 3* below, *Being Brilliant and standing out from the crowd.*

If you have gaps in experience and knowledge, do not ignore them. Identify and address them positively. *Section 4: Addressing gaps in knowledge, experience and skills* covers this in more detail.

v. Identify the application requirements

Lastly, make sure you provide everything that is required in the application details. For example, they may ask for references, a covering letter and proof of qualifications. If you do not provide everything they ask for in the way they ask for it, your application is going to be rejected.

If you are uncertain of the requirements, ask!

3. Being *Brilliant* and standing out from the crowd

By now you know what you need to put in your CV and how to go about structuring it. The next stage is writing it so you stand out from the crowd, grabbing the reader's attention early... in those vital first few seconds of their scanning your CV. How do you do this?

i. Choose the right CV format

ii. Identify your unique selling points – your USPs

iii. Use action words

iv. Use positive language

i. Choose the right CV format for you

Make sure the format of CV you use is going to work for you. Should you be using a skills-based CV rather than a chronological one? Would a hybrid CV get their attention faster than a chronological one? Choose the format of CV that will get you noticed fast.

ii. Your unique selling points - your USPs

You need to identify the achievements, skills, knowledge and experience that are unique to you and relevant to the job you are applying for. For example, you may be great at snake-charming but if it isn't relevant to that solicitors' office administrator role you are applying for, then it shouldn't be included! However, if you were applying for a role in a pet shop that specialises in reptiles then it could be a fantastic USP.

Your USPs are those pieces of work you have done that demonstrate how good you are at what you do. They don't have to be large special projects, they can just as easily be that extra effort – that extra mile – you put into your everyday job that has made a real difference, has achieved something extra and has been recognised by others as a great piece of work.

Recognising our USPs can be hard as we don't like to blow our own trumpets. We may believe it is inappropriate to say just how good we are. But think for a moment… How will your prospective employer know what you have achieved and what you can do unless you tell them? They can't read your mind, or between the lines of your CV!

If you are finding it hard to identify your key achievements, ask colleagues and look back at appraisals and feedback that you have had. What are you most proud of?

Once you have identified your USPs, you need to write them in a succinct and clear way, enabling the reader to see exactly what you have done. Each one should be a simple bullet point, outlined in no more than 2 or 3 sentences.

Some examples:

- *'Negotiated the best position for ABC Council, its community and its partners. This included the negotiation of grant reductions whilst avoiding adverse publicity, persuading staff and members on specific pieces of policy implementation and ensuring that we had a voice in county-wide projects.' (Manager, Local Government)*

- *'Opened many bank accounts through personal recommendations from satisfied customers who appreciated the competent, open and honest approach adopted.' (Financial Services Administrator)*

- *'Identified and recorded risks and issues, recommending solutions, increasing efficiency by 20%.' (Internal Auditor)*

iii. Use action words

When writing your CV, use action words. These are active, positive words – usually verbs – that give additional impact to what you are saying and make a stronger impression on the reader – your potential employer.

Action words should be used to convey what you have achieved – not just the tasks you have carried out.

For example, you may write:

*'As part of my role, I **had to** carry out a survey of customer's attitudes to services provided at the call centre. This **involved** interviewing customers by phone and email. A database **was used** to keep track of data collected. This project was **finished** on time and **used** to make changes to the customer experience.'*

But consider the greater impact, if you wrote:

*'**Devised** and **prepared** a survey of customer's attitudes to services provided at the call centre to **assess** what changes could be made to **increase** customer satisfaction. **Interviewed** 100 customers and **obtained** a substantial amount of data. **Created** a database to **analyse** and **interpret** this material in a format that could be easily read. **Completed** this project three weeks ahead of schedule and **established** key areas for improvement, thereby **influencing** the changes to be made to the services.'*

The action words above are more descriptive and give a real feel for what was done and what was achieved. They also give a greater impression of the writer – an impression of a positive, motivated person who knows how to present themselves in a businesslike way. The reader is more likely to see this person as someone who could succeed in a variety of work areas.

Review your CV. Could it do with more action words?

More examples of action words can be found in Annex B of this booklet.

iv. Use positive language

By using positive language, we come across as more positive, motivated and professional. This is language that – like using action words – describes what we have achieved in a proactive, beneficial and positive way. It creates a positive impact on the reader.

For example, you could write:

'Took over and turned around a failing team who were not performing due to previous poor team leadership and decision-making.'

Consider this instead:

'Worked with and motivated my new team through organisational and process changes to increase our efficiency and effectiveness, making legacy issues a thing of the past.'

This latter version gives the impression of someone who is proactive, forward-looking and a team player.

It is the language we use that makes the difference between something sounding positive or negative. Review what you have written and make sure you are giving the right impression. There are always ways and means of saying something in a positive way.

Positive language Tips: Using 'but' and 'however' can create a negative sentence. Consider changing them to 'and'. For example, consider the different impressions of the following:

'The project was challenging **but** I succeeded through sound planning and regular meetings.'

Or:

'The project was challenging **and** I succeeded through sound planning and regular meetings.'

4. Addressing gaps in knowledge, experience and skills

When matching your own skills and experience to the job requirements, you may find you have gaps. It is very rare for someone to meet every single requirement and other applicants may also have gaps. Success ingetting an interview depends on what those gaps are and how they have been addressed in your application.

Prospective employers are looking for people who meet the main criteria with solid, relevant experience and have the right personal qualities. If you offer other desirable qualities and experience, then that will further support your application. However, if essential skills and experience are missing, it is very unlikely that you will be asked for an interview. So address those gaps!

The first thing is to check if your gaps are key to the job's requirements. Sometimes the job description includes a person specification that will indicate if a particular requirement is essential or desirable. If your gap is desirable then you don't have to worry so much about addressing it in your CV. If it is essential, it is crucial that you do cover it in your CV.

It can be very tempting to skirt over or completely ignore gaps, hoping that no-one will notice! Unfortunately, unaddressed gaps stand out like sore thumbs and empty statements can damage your credibility.

So what do we do with these gaps?

When coaching my clients, I get them to fully explore their gaps, reading the job requirements and understanding exactly what is being asked for. Then I ask them the following questions, which you should ask of yourself, noting down your answers:

- What experience do you actually have?

- What knowledge do you have?

- What have you done in previous roles that could be relevant? Think about transferable skills and experience.

- What experience do you have through other activities that you are involved in? For example, if team leadership experience is required, have you led in the Scouts or Guides? If the role includes chairing committees, maybe you have done something similar in a voluntary role, perhaps as a parish councillor or trustee of a charitable organisation? Think outside the box.

- What would you do to fill that gap once you were in the role? Think of an example where you have taken on a new responsibility or started a new job and you have had gaps in key areas of experience or knowledge. What did you do to get that experience and knowledge so you could fulfil your responsibilities successfully? We all have experience of filling gaps.

Using your answers to the above questions, how much of a gap do you really have?

Use this information to address those gaps, stating them as a positive rather than stating them as a gap. For example, suppose project management was one of a number of key requirements of the role you were applying for. You have never managed a project before and this is a gap. Having gone through the questions above, you realise that you have a PRINCE2 qualification and have been involved in a number of projects in the various roles you have held. This has given you a sound understanding of how successful projects are managed and run. The only thing you haven't done is manage a project yourself.

One way you could write this is:

'Although I don't have all the experience you are looking for in project management, I have studied PRINCE2 and have been involved in many projects in previous roles that have given me an understanding of how projects are managed.'

A much better way of writing it would be:

'I am qualified in PRINCE2 and have a sound understanding and knowledge of project management, supported by solid experience of working in challenging and successful projects. For example...'

Here, you are focusing the reader on those aspects of your experience that match the requirements of the role. Your prospective employer can see that you have all the qualifications and knowledge and, without you actually having to state it, you just haven't managed a project yet. If your other skills and experience make you a good candidate for the role, your prospective employer could invite you for interview and then ask you competency-based questions around how you would go about managing a project. After all, we all have to do things for a first time!

> ## Never lie or fabricate information on your CV. You will be found out!

5. Before you send your *Brilliant* CV in...

These are my top tips to do before you send in your *Brilliant CV*:

✓ Once completed, leave your CV to one side for a day or two and then re-read it. You will be amazed at what you find to correct, change and even add.

✓ Get someone else to read it to make sure it all makes sense.

✓ Ask others if it conveys what you want it to. Do you come across in the way you want to?

✓ Check it for typos and grammatical errors. Don't rely on the computer to do this as the computer will not highlight incorrect words that are spelt correctly. If this is not your strong area, ask someone who is good at checking documents.

✓ Check it for style consistency, e.g. the use of capital letters, bullets, font styles and sizes, commas and semi-colons.

✓ Print it out to ensure it looks okay. It also means you have a hard copy as backup.

✓ If you have written your CV in something other than a Windows application (Word being the most common), check what system the organisation you are sending it to operates in and ensure your CV is compatible. Make sure it opens up properly and in the right format.

✓ Remember to write your covering letter and/or email with as much care as your CV (see Chapter 6).

✓ Check you have fully understood all the application requirements and your submission complies.

✓ Give yourself lots of time. Do not send it in with only a few moments until the deadline. Complete your CV and have it all checked with time to spare. Therefore, if anything goes wrong when uploading onto the Job Site, emailing the organisation or agency, or even with the good old-fashioned postal service, you have time to put it right.

✓ Send your CV to a real person and keep a copy. This ensures you have someone to call to check that it has been received okay and to follow up with.

✓ If you are posting a hard copy, you may want to print it out double-sided. However, the risk with this is that the reader may not turn it over, assuming you have sent in only a single page! Make sure there is a PTO (please turn over) in the bottom right-hand corner of the page.

✓ Also ensure you are using a good quality paper.

My Top tips for *BRILLIANT* CVs

✓ Most people only scan the first page and may or may not delve onto the next! You need to grab their attention early.

✓ Keep the layout clear and simple, so information can easily be found. Be succinct and to the point – your information needs to stand out.

✓ Make sure your CV is tailored to their requirements.

✓ Stand out from the crowd by including examples of key achievements that are your USPs.

✓ Use their language where you can.

✓ The standard length for the CV is two pages.

✓ Don't use flashy fonts or designs.

✓ Make sure your spelling, punctuation and grammar are perfect – get it checked.

✓ Most employers need to check for gaps in employment history so help with this by keeping all your dates to the right of the CV.

✓ Your CV should sell you to the employer, so be as positive as possible and never lie.

✓ Make sure you send it to a real person and keep a copy!

✓ When emailing or uploading your CV, give yourself plenty of time. Don't leave it to the deadline as lots of other people will be doing the same and might cause their systems to slow down or crash. If this happens or anything else goes wrong, you want to give yourself plenty of time to try again before the deadline.

FINAL WORDS ON YOUR BRILLIANT CV... FEEDBACK...

Having written a great CV that shows you at your best, there may still be reasons beyond your control that mean you don't get an interview. Don't despair... Other candidates may have more relevant experience, greater knowledge or personal skills that you, as yet, don't have. HOWEVER, it is really important that you get feedback on why you didn't get through to an interview so you can learn from the experience and:

- ensure you have written your best possible CV and there was nothing else you could have done

- have an opportunity to understand areas where you can strengthen your CV for the next time

- manage your confidence, knowing there was nothing else you could have done and move onto your next application and interview.

CHAPTER 4
BRILLIANT TIPS TO DEAL WITH COMMON ISSUES WITH CVs

In this chapter, I look at 4 common issues that people struggle with when writing their CVs. These are:

1. Long-term absences from the job market

2. Employment gaps

3. A very long employment history

4. Changing careers/downsizing

1. Long-term absences from the job market

If you are coming back to work after a long absence, you **can** write a CV that gets you interviews.

The first thing to think about is why you have been absent for as long as you have and how would a prospective employer look at this. Common gaps include time out to raise a family, going back to college, living abroad, travelling and long-term unemployment. These gaps can easily be covered in a CV and, with a well-thought-out covering letter, can focus the reader on what you will bring to the role rather than your long-term absence from the job market.

If you feel your reason for absence from the job market may be an issue, for example, a long-term health issue that you have recovered from, or a term at Her Majesty's pleasure, I would recommend contacting someone responsible for recruitment in the organisation to talk through your situation. In these circumstances, they may be able to give you some advice on how to cover your absence in your application and specify any additional information they may need to help review your application. If they tell you that it is not worth applying, then it has saved you a lot of time and energy completing your application only to have your confidence dented by not getting through. This ensures that you apply for jobs in organisations that will consider you and give you an opportunity to get an interview (as long as your application is well thought out, clearly written and relevant).

Whatever the reason for your long-term absence, you must include it and never lie.

So what kind of CV would I recommend? In this instance, I would recommend the *skills-based CV* as this focuses your prospective employer's attention on how your skills and experience match the role rather than on your employment gap. For more information on the *skills-based CV*, see Chapter 2 and an example is in Annex C.

Describing your employment absence in your CV

It is important that you write your employment absence in a way that helps the reader assess your gap in a positive light. Sometimes this just needs to be a single entry as it tells them all they need to know quickly, allowing them to move on to your career history. For example:

Career Break (Young Family)	**2009 to date**

Or:

Career Break	**2012 to date**
Studying at Southampton University: Psychology Degree, completing July 2015	

However, your break may include great skills and experience that you want to show, demonstrating that you are still 'working'. For example, if during your gap you are doing voluntary work, perhaps a variety of part-time work, work experience and so forth, you should expand your entry.

For example:

Career Break   **2012 to date**

Following redundancy in 2009, held a number of part-time roles whilst seeking a full-time role. These roles enabled me to keep up to date with the industry and work practices.

Or:

Career Break   **2012 to date**

Following redundancy in 2009, have worked for local voluntary organisation taking on responsibilities for:

• Fundraising, including setting up and running stands at local shopping centres
• Working as part of a team responsible for clearing unsafe ground and making it into useable community areas.

Concerns that a prospective employer may have

When putting your CV together, put yourself in the reader's position. Why would they invite you to an interview? Why would they consider employing you? Ask yourself, 'Why should I employ me?' What are your answers? If they are a bit woolly... 'I am a great person'... you need to think about the facts of your skills and experience and how you can bring those to life for the reader.

With a long-term absence from the job market, an employer will naturally have some concerns and questions:

•   How recent is your experience?

•   Are you up to date with latest practice?

- Do you know the new regulations?

- Is your knowledge up to date?

- How would you fit into the working environment of today? And so forth.

It is important to think of these concerns and others, and to address them through your CV and covering letter. For example:

- If you are a professional, you should include how you keep yourself up to date with your profession. Maybe mention latest practice to demonstrate this.

- If you are a skilled person in the building trade, for example, you should include how you have kept your skills sharp and up to date; give a real example of what you have done.

- If you are an administrator or office worker, you should demonstrate how you have kept your IT and office skills up to date.

How would a prospective employer know, from your CV, that you would pick up the knowledge and skills required to do the job you are applying for easily and competently?

2. Employment gaps

Here we talk about those gaps in employment that are in our past.

If your gaps are for a few months, when you have been searching for a job, these tend to disappear in the CV. This is because we normally use years when dating roles. For example, if your previous role was from September 2004 to February 2006 and your next role didn't start until July 2006, your employment gap is between March and June 2006. If you are still in the role, the dates on your CV would be:

Current role dated 2006 to date

Previous role dated 2004 to 2006

This loses your 3-month gap.

This is usually acceptable. However, there may be times when it is important for all gaps to be included. For example, if you are applying for a role where it is essential that your employment record is checked for legal reasons or you have a criminal record. The latter must be disclosed. An employer may also ask for months to be included when dating your career roles.

Don't fear your gaps. Address them!

If your gap is longer than a year, this will create a gap in your career history. It is important that the gap is addressed so employers know what you have done. If it is just left as a gap, employers will wonder why it is there and could make an assumption that you are hiding something even if you are not.

Gaps can be for a variety of reasons, for example, raising a family, studying or travelling. Here, you just need to include it as one line in your CV at the appropriate point in your career history, giving a brief description. Gaps such as these can often add depth to us as a person and give the employer a greater impression of us.

If you have a number of gaps in your CV, take a moment to think about the impression this may give to the reader. This will help you to decide how you are going to write about those gaps.

For example, if all your gaps are for travelling and seem to happen every few years or so, the reader may be forgiven for wondering if you are someone who really wants the job or if you are just looking for a means of funding your next adventure!

If, however, your gaps are for different reasons then this could tell a story about you as a person. For example, you may have had a gap year early on in your working life, travelling as a young person, followed by a gap raising a family and perhaps a gap going back to college to get that degree. There is a maturity to this CV that tells a positive story of the person.

41

3. A very long employment history

The standard practice for CVs is for them to be no more than 2 pages long. People with long career histories often struggle to convey their experience in such a short space. However, people I have worked with have been amazed at how easy it actually is to get everything you need into 2 pages and I hope the following hints, tips and guidance will help you create your own 2-page CV.

Firstly, remember:

- your CV is not there to tell your career's life history, it is there to highlight key skills and achievements, to grab the attention of the reader and to get you an interview

- your early career is almost certainly not relevant to the role you are applying for as you will have moved on significantly since then

- most employers are normally only interested in what you have been doing in the last 10 years or so, with the emphasis on your most recent role(s)

- your education becomes less important so you don't need to list every single 'O' level, 'A' level, CSE, GCSE, etc.

Writing your early career

One way of writing your early career is to just list your roles under the heading 'Early Career' on page 2 of your CV. For example, if you were a senior manager in the retail sector, your early career may look like the following:

Early Career

Sales Manager	ABC Shop Ltd	1997 – 2000
Sales Assistant Manager	ABC Shop Ltd	1995 – 1997
Sales Assistant	Grocers plc	1992 – 1994
Sales Assistant	Sports Shop Ltd	1990 – 1991

An alternative way of writing the above would be:

Early Career   **1990 - 2000**

During my early career, I worked my way up from a sales assistant at Sports Shop Ltd to Sales Manager at ABC Shop Ltd in 1997, before moving on to my first senior manager role in 2000.

If your early career was with a single organisation, you could head up a paragraph similar to the one above with:

Early Retail Career with ABC Ltd   **1990 - 2000**

I joined ABC Ltd in 1990 as a sales assistant, was promoted to Assistant Manager in 1995 and then Sales Manager in 1997 before taking up my first senior manager post in 2000.

4. Changing careers or downsizing

People who are looking to change careers and, in particular, downsize their careers, often wonder how to write their CV so that they are considered as a credible candidate.

For anyone in this situation, I recommend writing a *skills-based* CV as it focuses the recruiter on how you match the role before they look at your career history. If you have succeeded in grabbing their interest on page 1, the impact of your career background may be lessened.

More information on the *skills-based* CV is in Chapter 2 and all the information on writing your CV in Chapter 3 is relevant for you.

When changing careers, it is your transferable skills, experience and knowledge that will sell you into an interview. It is important that you identify these and write them in a succinct, credible and relevant way, using the language of the organisation to show how your experience translates across from your current role.

Each sector, industry and organisation has its own jargon and terminology. If you use the jargon from your previous/current role in your CV, you may run the risk of not being understood by the reader. As a result, they may find it too difficult to read, may not be able to match your skills and experience to their requirements and your application will fail. Use plain English and ask someone to check what you have written for understanding.

Addressing employers' concerns

If you are changing your career, you will be up against people who may have relevant industry/sector experience. How do you convince a prospective employer to engage you rather than someone who already works in the field?

If you are downsizing your career, you need to assure the reader that you are not overqualified for the role. They may wonder why someone such as you would be applying for a role at that level. They will be concerned that you would get bored or try to take over. So it is important that you address these concerns in your application.

Put yourself in the recruiter's shoes and ask yourself, 'Why would I consider my application?' 'Would I interview me for this role just based on my CV and covering letter?'

Covering letters are important for explaining why we are applying for a role and conveying why the reader should consider us for interview. If you feel you would like to know more about writing successful covering letters, I have provided my top tips for writing covering letters in Chapter 6. In addition, my booklet *Your Brilliant Covering Letters & Emails* looks at these in more detail and provides letter templates.

CHAPTER 5

A BRILLIANT CV STYLE THAT WORKS: THE HYBRID CV IN MORE DETAIL

The CV that my clients have found very successful, and employers seem to like, is the *hybrid CV*. The format of this CV allows the reader to quickly and easily determine if the applicant is a candidate worth considering as it brings together the *skills-based CV* and the *chronological CV*.

The only time I would not recommend this CV is if you need to highlight your transferable skills rather than your career history. For example, when changing careers, coming back after a long absence or if it is your first job. Here the skills-based CV does the job better.

Below I take you through each part of the *hybrid CV*, which you should read in conjunction with the example of a *hybrid CV* in Annex C. We will look at:

page 1 of the CV:

- Personal details
- Your profile
- Skills and attributes
- Career

page 2 of the CV:

- Career continued
- Professional qualifications, training and education

I hope these notes will guide you through writing your own *hybrid* CV.

Please be aware that the following notes assume you are creating a Word document.

Page 1 of the CV

Annex C has an example of a real *hybrid* CV and demonstrates each section that is covered below. Use the example in conjunction with the text below and it will be easier to follow.

- **Personal details:** Your name should be included in the header of the document so it appears on each page. Your contact details should be placed at the top of page 1 so they can be found easily by anyone who needs to refer to them. This includes your address, contact telephone number(s) and contact email address.

Contact Information Tips:

Email: Check your email address. If you are using a family address, just make sure it is something sensible. For example, yummymummy4@ themadhouse.net may not be giving the impression you want to give to a prospective employer! If this sounds familiar, think about opening a Hotmail or Google or other generic email account.

Voicemail: If you are giving personal phone numbers as contact details, it may be worth checking your home and mobile phone voicemail messages that callers hear!

Facebook: Could a prospective employer get access to you or your family's Facebook page? If they could, what would it say about you? Employers are increasingly looking here for information on applicants.

Twitter: If you have a Twitter account, what would it tell a prospective employer about you if they signed up to follow you?

- **Your profile:** At the top of page 1, beneath your contact details, you should write a short paragraph that succinctly describes who you are in your professional capacity. This is your profile and provides the reader with an instant impression of you, your experience and background. It is important that this profile is tailored to the requirements of the role you are applying for. For example:

'An events manager with strong organisational and administrative skills and experienced in providing a quality service to the client. Accustomed to working under pressure and using her initiative.'

'A commercially aware Finance Director with experience of developing systems in a rapidly expanding and changing company, covering FMCG, manufacturing and project management. Strongly analytical, quick to grasp and understand the detail. A pragmatic hands-on attitude and flexible approach to problem-solving.'

- **Skills and attributes:** Immediately following your profile, you should bullet point your core skills that meet the key requirements of the role. These core skills allow the reader to assess very quickly if you are a credible candidate for the role and encourage them to read the rest of your CV.

These skills should be tailored to the role you are applying for and should be around 5 in total. They should be bulleted with a heading in bold, followed by a brief description that brings each skill to life, thereby making them credible. Some examples:

- Change management – Fundamental role in continual process to maintain and improve the organisation's performance through initiatives to implement 'best practice' processes, including a full understanding of the people aspects of change

- Organisational skills – Highly organised with experience of working in a highly pressurised customer-focused environment, working to tight deadlines with a need for accuracy

- **Career:** After your skills summary, you should start to summarise your career. To help the reader navigate their way around the CV, I recommend you put a heading such as 'Career', which is then followed by your current role. It is important that your current role is contained on page 1 of your CV as this is the one that your prospective employer will be most interested in. Try hard not to let your summary go on to Page 2, as the reader may just assume it ends at the bottom of Page 1 and miss important details.

To summarise your current role, I recommend that you start with a heading, putting your job title on the left followed by the organisation's name and then the dates you were there. For example:

Customer Services Supervisor   Insurance plc   2010 to date

Your role heading should be in bold to indicate it is a heading. It will also attract the attention of the reader as they scan the document.

Your role heading should be followed by a succinct paragraph, summarising your responsibilities. This should include, as appropriate:

- your main responsibilities as relevant to the role you are applying for

- the number of people/teams you manage or supervise

- the size of the budget you manage in £s

- the title of the person you report to. If you hold a senior role, state if you report to the Board, the Chief Executive or perhaps a Board of Trustees.

This paragraph should be followed by 3 to 5 bulleted examples of your key achievements. This is your opportunity to highlight your unique selling points and stand out from the crowd, demonstrating your relevant experience in a credible and succinct way.

Your key achievements should be bulleted, brief and tailored to the requirements of the role you are applying for. For examples, look at both the chronological and hybrid CVs in Annex C.

Page 2 of the CV

Annex C has an example of a real hybrid CV and demonstrates each section that is covered below. Use the example in conjunction with the text below and it will be easier to follow.

- **Career continued:** The rest of your career should be on page 2, with roles within the last 10 years summarised in the same way as your current role. Jobs held over 10 years ago can be summarised under a heading, 'Early Career'. There is no need to go into detail for these jobs as you will have moved on considerably since then. The only exception I would make is if there is something in your early career that is very relevant to the role you are applying for, or if it helps to fill a gap.

> **Remember** - you only need to put enough in your CV to win you the interview. Anything else is superfluous and if the organisation wants to know more they can ask you in the interview.

- **Professional qualifications, training and education:** These should be placed on page 2 of your CV, after your career. They should be summarised with your latest qualifications first.

  The order should be professional qualifications, followed by training at work, university or college and then school. Note that the older you get, the less detail you need to put in about school and qualifications. Here, early education can be summarised.

  If you are a school leaver or graduate, then it is important that you list your qualifications and grades so your prospective employer can see what you have achieved.

  Dates when you qualified should be shown and, as with your career details, these dates should be listed on the right-hand side.

- **Interests:** Some people include interests and some people don't. The benefit of having an interests section is it gives you an opportunity to show something of who you are as a person, creating a more rounded view of you. This is also a great section to bring in voluntary work and hobbies, which involve other skills and interests that add another dimension to who you are, for example, being a scout or guide leader, project managing a building project or writing articles for local papers. I would shy away from interests such as watching TV, going to the pub with friends and eating out. I would also think hard before putting in high-risk interests unless, of course, it is relevant to the role you are applying for. Having said that, in a previous life, saying I was part of a hot-air balloon team didn't stop me securing a role in a financial services plc as an Audit Manager! It can create intrigue and help you stand out from the crowd.

- **References:** This is a usual requirement for Public Sector applications, but is not normally done in the Private Sector unless specifically asked for. Where required, it is standard to give two referees – people who can give their opinion on your abilities. Please ensure you ask their permission before adding them to your CV.

Please note that it is not a requirement to include your date of birth, age, sex or your marital status in your CV.

CHAPTER 6
HINTS & TIPS FOR BRILLIANT COVERING LETTERS

Below I have given you my top hints and tips for writing successful covering letters. These are relevant whether you are writing a Word document to be sent in as an attachment, a hard-copy letter to be posted, or setting it all out in an email. More information on covering letters and emails, together with templates, can be found in my booklet, *Your Brilliant Covering Letters & Emails*.

My 12 top tips for writing Brilliant covering letters

1. Each covering letter should be tailored to the job application.

2. Keep it simple and to the point.

3. Personalise your letter; address it to a real person.

4. Put the job reference and title on the letter.

5. In the main body of the letter:

   a. start by briefly explaining why you are writing to them

   b. next, explain why you are applying for the role, telling them how you match what they are looking for. Include experience and qualifications

   c. provide a couple of examples of key achievements that demonstrate how you match the role and grab their attention.

6. Use bullet points to create the maximum impact with as few words as possible, helping the reader to quickly see what you have written.

7. Be positive, proactive and enthusiastic.

8. In the final paragraph, point the addressee to your CV that you have attached for consideration.

9. Finally, thank the person for their time and consideration, stating that

you are looking forward to hearing from them and having an opportunity to find out more about the organisation and the role in the interview.

10.   Close with your full name and signature.

11.   Ensure your contact details are on the letter as well as on your CV.

12.   Keep a copy of your letter, together with your CV and any other information submitted ready for that interview, so they can be used for the interview and as a basis for other applications.

Use this checklist to ensure you have done everything you can to make your CV stand out and maximise your chances of securing that interview.

Have you:

YOUR BRILLIANT CV CHECKLIST		DONE ✓
1	read all of the information around the role, identifying the essential requirements?	
2	checked you fully understand the key requirements and are not making any assumptions?	
3	matched your skills, experience, knowledge and capabilities to the role?	
4	identified any gaps you have in the required skills, knowledge and experience and know how you are going to address them in your application?	
5	identified your unique selling points and key achievements?	
6	decided on a format of CV that will work for you?	
7	ensured your CV is only 2 pages long?	
8	included dates and made it easy for the reader to follow the chronological order of your jobs, training and education?	
9	identified any employment gaps and how you are going to address them?	

YOUR BRILLIANT CV CHECKLIST		DONE ✓
10	read it through to make sure it makes sense and is completely relevant, if you are editing from a previous CV?	
11	given yourself time to leave it for a few days and then go back to check it?	
12	given yourself enough time to submit your CV, allowing for any technical problems or unexpected delays?	
13	checked for typos, grammatical errors, inappropriate jargon, etc.?	
14	checked how the recruiter wants to receive your CV and in what format?	
15	done a covering letter?	
16	kept a copy of everything you are sending in?	

accomplished	converted	established
achieved	coordinated	estimated
administered	corrected	evaluated
advised	created	examined
analysed	cut	expanded
approved		explained
arranged	decreased	facilitated
assessed	defined	forecast
assisted	delivered	formulated
attained	demonstrated	founded
	designed	
budgeted	determined	generated
built	developed	guided
brokered	devised	grew
	diagnosed	gathered
calculated	directed	
captured	discovered	identified
centralised	distributed	impacted
checked	documented	implemented
collected	doubled	improved
combined	drove	improvised
completed		increased
composed	earned	initiated
conceived	edited	inspired
conducted	eliminated	installed
consolidated	encouraged	instigated
consulted	engineered	instructed
controlled	ensured	interpreted

introduced

launched
led
liaised

machined
maintained
managed
marketed
modernised
monitored
motivated

negated
negotiated

obtained
operated
organised

performed
persuaded
planned
prepared
presented
processed
promoted

recommended
redesigned

reduced
reorganised
represented
researched
resolved
responsible for
reviewed
revised

scheduled
selected
sold
solved
specified
standardised
started
strengthened
structured
supervised
supported

taught
tested
trained
translated

uncovered
utilised

verified
valued

widened
won

ANNEX C - CV EXAMPLES

1. Example of a skills-based CV - John Hyde

This CV is based on an HR professional's CV who had been made redundant from a Public Sector organisation. They had registered with a local job agency but weren't being put forward for jobs that they knew they were a good candidate for. As soon as they redid their CV as a skills-based CV, they were, within a matter of weeks, put forward for a Private Sector position and got that job! The agency said they hadn't realised just how experienced they were! Their perception had been clouded by the Public Sector tag attached to their exceptional experience.

2. Example of a chronological CV - Sam Smith

This CV is based on a Financial Services administrator looking to stay in the industry and get a similar role. In this instance, the chronological CV works really well for them as the reader can see immediately the level and relevance of their experience.

3. Example of a hybrid CV - Jane White

This CV is based on a Web and Communications Manager's CV who was seeking a role in web management and was not so interested in the organisation or sector within which it was based. Here, combining the skills summary with their latest role gave them a flexible CV that they could tailor across a number of different organisations. This person moved from the Education Sector into a Private Sector organisation, specialising in web management.

John Hyde

63 High Street Somerton Wilts SR12 6RT
Telephone: 01245 0123456 Email: johnhyde@email.co.uk

A qualified HR Business Partner with extensive practical experience of strategic and operational Human Resources management. I have a positive and enthusiastic outlook and excellent communication skills that have enabled me to build strong and effective working relationships with different stakeholders. Customer focused and results driven, I have worked in partnership with senior managers to successfully deliver major change projects in complex and unionised operating environments.

KEY SKILLS AND AREAS OF EXPERTISE

Change management:
Very experienced in delivering complex change programmes. E.g., as part of the HR project team leading on the merger of five different organisations (15,000 employees through TUPE transfer), worked alongside managers to proactively address the challenges of the new organisation. Including, redesigning structures, team and job roles; challenging operating models; relocating employees; negotiating changes to terms and conditions and working practices.

Employee relations:
Adept at creating collaborative working relationships with different stakeholders, including managers and Trade Union representatives, enabling me to influence others and deliver change successfully. E.g., I negotiated and implemented new terms and conditions, including the introduction of bank holiday working to the Waste Collection workforce with 100% engagement.

Project management:
PRINCE2-qualified project manager with excellent organisational and forward-planning skills. Able to co-ordinate others and deliver to a high standard. I have worked in partnership with managers to implement business projects to strict deadlines. E.g., working with the business to redesign job roles and reduce the number of management posts, we achieved £2million of savings.

Employment law:
Excellent knowledge of U.K. employment law and best practice with the ability to apply this knowledge to achieve business objectives. E.g., I advised the Chief Executive on the HR policy and process for merging two service directorates, implementing a redundancy process which resulted in £1M of savings.

Team management:
Experienced people manager who has led a team of HR Advisors to provide a first-class, customer-focused HR service, supporting 2000 employees. Also work effectively and collaboratively as part of an HR and OD management team.

Innovation and creativity:
Responsive to business needs with a 'can do' approach, applying a bespoke solution to their requirements. E.g., used this approach successfully to introduce new terms and conditions to a highly unionised workforce, with the potential to cause major service disruption and reputational issues for the business. These changes were delivered on time with 100% engagement of the 260-strong workforce.

HR strategy:
Adept at developing strategic working relationships with managers, which has enabled me to actively promote changes in HR through the adoption of a different operating model that is based on a 'value' added HR service with managers being encouraged to use online tools to resolve straightforward people issues.

John Hyde

CAREER SUMMARY

HR Business Partner, ADC Council, Bath   **2009 – date**
Responsible for working with senior managers across the business to transform their services, plan for the future, manage change and the implementation of complex projects to increase customer satisfaction, improve efficiency and achieve ambitious financial savings.

HR Manager, East Somerton District Council, Somerton (ESDC)   **2008 – 2009**
Responsible for the management of the HR, learning and development, and facilities management functions of the Council. Additionally, as the HR representative from ESDC on the local government reorganisation project, I worked as part of the team developing policy, managing employee relation issues, staff consultation and managing change.

Principal HR Officer, East Somerton District Council, Somerton   **2004 – 2008**
Responsible for the management of the HR and learning and development functions, providing a service that included delivering a people strategy, research and development of people policies, managing employee relation issues, recruitment and selection, job evaluation, provision of workforce data and equalities and diversity.

HR Officer, East Somerton District Council, Somerton   **2000 – 2004**
Provided a comprehensive HR advisory service to the organisation. As an HR officer, I provided support to managers on all people issues including grievance, disciplinary, sickness absence, capability and redundancy.

Personnel Assistant, ABC Recruitment Ltd, Bath   **1999 – 2000**
Responsible for the co-ordination of recruitment activity, including writing recruitment advertisements, managing applications, producing contracts of employment and coordinating graduate recruitment and staff induction.

Recruitment Consultant, Direct Recruitment, Bath   **1998 – 1999**
The recruitment agency specialised in providing qualified LGV drivers to organisations and it was my responsibility to recruit new drivers, source new work and allocate drivers to assignments on a daily basis.

PROFESSIONAL QUALIFICATIONS & CPD
- Chartered Member of the CIPD   **2003**
- Postgraduate Diploma in Human Resources Management
  University of the West of England   **2003**
- PRINCE2 Project Management Certificate   **2008**
- Certificate in Personnel Practice, City of Bath College   **2000**

EDUCATION
- BA Hons in Drama, Theatre Studies and English, University of Surrey   **1997**
- 3 A levels and 9 GCSEs (including Mathematics and English)   **1994**
  The John of Gaunt School, Bristol

KEY IT SKILLS
   Word, Excel, PowerPoint, Internet, Email, Compel, SAP and TRIM (document management system)

SAM SMITH

21 Street Lane
Village
Salisbury, Wilts SP6 2BZ
Tel: 0111 055332
Email: samsmith@email.com

An efficient administrator and organiser with a background in financial services. Good interpersonal skills and wide experience in working with customers. Strong planning skills and efficient working manner, getting on with the job in hand and delivering what is required. Supervisory experience.

CAREER AT ABC BANK PLC

Business Account Manager   Salisbury Branch   2009 – 2012
Responsible for 150 business customers, meeting all their borrowing, investing and money management needs, working closely with managers of other financial disciplines in the bank. *Excellent understanding of all accounting procedures; interpreting management information (however presented!), audited accounts and cash flow projections.*

- Instrumental in persuading several large and prestigious local accounts to transfer to ABC

- Opened many accounts through personal recommendations from satisfied customers who appreciated the competent, open and honest approach adopted

Senior Lending Officer   Salisbury Branch   2006 – 2009
Working with senior Commercial Managers, as well as a short period as Customer Services Assistant. Customer liaison, processing applications, deputising in manager's absence. Building on knowledge of all business banking requirements.

Supervisor of Central Lending – Southampton (Pilot Project)   2004 – 2006
Initially under a dedicated Manager, but latterly working largely unsupervised. Running a unit of 5/6 clerks, successfully leading and motivating the team under difficult circumstances. Pilot declared successful and rolled out nationwide. Responsible for distribution of workload, ensuring standards maintained and deadlines met. Assisting and advising colleagues; production and distribution of a Newsletter. Direct input to staff appraisals.

Senior Counsellor   Totton Branch   2002 – 2004
Control of all personal lending. A fair and firm approach, resulting in many recovery situations. Success in this role led to Supervisor position shown above.

SAM SMITH

EARLY CAREER

Various Bank Branches   **1990 – 1992**
Worked at Winchester, Salisbury and Romsey branches in customer-facing roles.
Secretarial work, sales support, and area support for special projects/promotions.
Presentations to staff re achieving targets. Organising Bank presence at outside
events (Romsey Show, freshers' fairs, etc.).

Prior to employment with ABC Bank, worked for sole practitioner Solicitor on one-to-
one basis, and in an Architectural practice. Both provided good background
experience and information for later work.

EDUCATION/QUALIFICATIONS

10 GCE 'O' Levels
London Chamber of Commerce – Private Secretary's Certificate
RSA Typing and Shorthand
Word and Excel experience
'Negotiation Skills' and 'Winning New Business' courses

PERSONAL

Acted as Executor for the Wills of three family members, obtaining Probate/Letters of
Administration, collecting and distributing the entire Estates.

Interests: Volunteering in our community shop, garden design and drawing

Jane White

25 The Road, The Town, Oxfordshire OX01 6XX
tel: 00112 123456 email: janewhite@email.com
portfolio: www.myportfolio.com

Profile summary

Conscientious, professionally qualified design manager with over ten years' experience in developing comprehensive web and communication strategies. Multi-talented across marketing, web and graphic design. A record of producing creative projects with high attention to detail, tight deadlines and budgets. Customer focused with strong interpersonal, leadership and project management skills.

Skills and attributes

- **Contract management:** experienced in preparing briefs, production schedules and negotiating contracts when commissioning design agencies, freelance photographers and authors.
- **Graphic design:** well versed in the entire design process from initial meetings with clients (external and internal), requirements-gathering, concepts and implementation to final artwork and print production. Expert knowledge of Adobe products and producing print-ready artwork; this includes InDesign, Illustrator and Photoshop. Has broad experience of producing web and print designs in a range of media, including magazines, direct mail campaigns, academic reports, online banner ads, website templates, business stationery, conference displays, classroom activity packs and teaching resources. Has an understanding of the capabilities and limitations of both web and print, and how they can integrate together to produce an effective campaign. Online portfolio: www.myportfolio.com
- **Brand identities:** devises brand identities for government projects by conducting brand workshops and researching customer personas. Co-ordinates the rolling out of the brand nationally to regional offices by issuing style guidelines. Ensures the identity is maintained by advising staff and signing off artwork.
- **Project management and leading teams:** successfully overseen the delivery of over 20 websites, including multimillion-pound government projects. Experienced in making business cases; preparing cost-benefit analysis; calculating break-even; writing and implementing project plans; and leading teams.

Career

Web and Communications Manager   **University of Wiltshire**   2002 – 2011
Subject Centre for Languages, Linguistics and Area Studies

Responsible for shaping the entire creative output, from websites to traditional print campaigns. Overseeing the creation of websites with simple, useable and attractive interfaces, using web standards (HTML and CSS), including interactive elements such as feedback/event registration. The role included planning and implementing marketing strategy, creating artwork for print collateral and publications together with online marketing. As part of this role, I spent six years (2002-2009) as the web editor of the Modern Languages and Film Studies websites. Currently manage a team of four (including two web developers and a graphic designer). Experienced at leading teams and line management, including writing job specifications; conducting interviews, inductions and appraisals; workload delegation; identifying opportunities for staff development; and annual leave. Skilled in adapting management style to suit individual members of staff; can motivate others and get the best from them.

Key achievements:

- **New product development**: as a new venture for the unit, spearheaded a marketing strategy to develop a series of products with the business objective to generate additional income to offset recent government budget cuts. The project involved customer research, cost-benefit and break-even analysis. The products have turned a profit of between 16-25%. Also created artwork for the products, examples can be found at www.pathsintolanguages.ac.uk
- **Design**: another example of design work is Liaison Magazine, a publication targeted at the Higher Education community. Defined the concept, designed and created artwork for the magazine. 80% of readers surveyed rated its visual appeal as 'excellent'. Examples can be found at www.uniwilt.ac.uk/news/newsletter.html
- Meeting targets: conducted a targeted marketing campaign to raise brand awareness that resulted in adding 10,000 teachers to the CRM system (Customer Relationship Management) within 18 months and meeting a key-performance indicator set by the funders.

Jane White

Web Editor   University of Wiltshire, Business Services   **2000 – 2002**
This role covered web responsibilities for the Catering Department, the Conference Office, and Travel & Accommodation Office, creating five customer-focused websites for this large, non-academic department of the University. Proposed the strategy for developing the multiple websites in tandem (timescales, content provision and photography). This resulted in promotion.

Administrative Assistant   University of Wiltshire, Business Services   **1998 – 2000**
This involved budget monitoring, preparing VAT returns, data analysis and the handling of confidential information. An understanding of the financial and legal implications of contracts was also required.

Finance Assistant   University of Wiltshire, Finance Department   **1997 – 1998**
The administration of research contracts funded by the European Commission, Research Councils and Industry. Experience in accounting software. Built up varied skills in financial management.

Visual Merchandiser   Debenhams, Hampshire   **1996 – 1997**

Professional qualifications and development

- Diploma in Digital Marketing, Chartered Institute of Marketing (CIM)   2011 (on-going)

  The qualification covers Search Engine Optimisation (SEO), Pay Per Click (PPC), types of online advertising, email marketing, viral marketing, online PR, affiliate marketing and social media. It also looks at digital metrics, legislation, regulation and codes of practice.
- Professional Diploma in Marketing, Chartered Institute of Marketing (CIM)   2009 – 2010

  Passed all four units: Marketing, Planning and Management, Project Management, Delivering Customer Value. Obtained a distinction (top 6%) for the report on marketing planning, and recognition by the college who requested it to be featured on their website as an example of outstanding work.
- Building and leading teams, University of Wiltshire, one-day course   2009
- Essential skills for new managers, University of Wiltshire, two-day course   2009
- Marketing for the Olympics, Chartered Institute of Marketing (CIM), one-day course   2009
- Web Directions @ Media Conference   2007 & 2008
- Macromedia Flash and Quark Express, Metropolitan University   2004
- Design principles for websites, University of Wiltshire   2000

Education

BA (Hons) Fine Art, 2:1
The Institute of Art and Design   1996
Diploma in Foundation Art and Design
Achieved the highest mark in year out of 100 students
Wiltshire School of Art   1993
3 A levels, City College   1992
9 GCSEs at grade A-C, including Mathematics and English   1990

Interests

Kitchen design, having completed four through to construction. Other interests include reading books on typography, planning road trips, walking, baking and all things Scandinavian.

www.ingramcontent.com/pod-product-compliance
Lightning Source LLC
Chambersburg PA
CBHW071609200326
41519CB00021BB/6941